One Funny Mummy Defines Parenthood

(in 140 Characters or Less)

Jewel Nunez

ISBN: 978-0-692-99182-4

Library of Congress Control Number available upon request.

Design and Cover by Lisa Forde

Printed in the United States of America
First printing December 2017

Published by OFM Inc.
onefunnymummy.com

For my girls
whom I love completely
and utterly
and without question

Introduction

I came to Twitter as a writer first and a parent second, but what I didn't realize was that being a parent led me to find my voice as a writer, at least when it came to writing tweets. My tweets are my honest take on parenting, and they're funny because they're true. But that's not to say I'm not kidding around. The "just kidding" is implied after each tweet I write. But I'm also kidding/not kidding, because most of what I write is true in some way. I think that's what people relate to: the truth inside the humor.

Since I joined Twitter, I've learned it's a temperamental place where at times it feels like you're in front of a firing squad of angry internet trolls who only want to bring you down. Write a couple tweets about your children and husband annoying you, and stand back for the inundation of hate comments that you're a terrible person and don't deserve your family. The great news is you can ignore them, knowing the people who say these things don't have a sense of humor and are totally miserable douche faces.

On the other hand, there are people who connect with your words in a way you never expected—the complete opposite of angry internet trolls. They're like supportive internet fairies, inspiring you to keep putting yourself and your words out there.

Not everyone will get my humor, but for those who understand, and even like it, I'm most grateful. I appreciate having a place to say what I want to about being a parent, and having other parents know what I mean, and sharing a laugh about the craziness that is parenthood.

Cheers,
OFM

Parenting is no different than a bear attack. Curl up and play dead, and they usually leave you alone.

It's so much fun being a parent. Everything you say is taken as a suggestion or simply ignored.

If you see me sleeping in my car, don't feel bad for me. I'm not homeless, just trying to get the fuck away from my kids.

If this kid's not gonna
nap, then she needs to
get a job.

You can't call yourself a mom until you've tried to poop faster 'cause a kid is screaming at you from the other room.

Parenting: negotiating with terrorists every single minute of every single day for the rest of your miserable life.

Having a little version
of yourself seems like
a good idea until you
realize how much of an
asshole you are.

This raising kids thing is really cutting into my me time.

I am woman, hear me complain about my routine only then to complain that I'm out of my routine.

Register for a new blender on your baby registry. It drowns out the crying and makes margaritas. You're welcome.

Problem of the Day

If a mom has 0 kids and 2 hours of free time, how long will she sit in the car looking at Twitter before entering Target?

Don't become a parent
if you don't want to feel
every emotion within
the first five minutes of
waking up.

You can still hear
your toddler from the
backseat.

-how to tell if your music
is too low.

Maybe instead of having a baby, you should just get a tattoo.

The only thing that gets me through the day is their sweet smiles.

Just kidding, it's the thought of them in bed and my full wine glass.

The baby said, "Hot Mama" ten times in a row. She was talking about her oatmeal, but I'll take what I can get.

If you let your kid be an asshole, don't be surprised when I treat him like one.

Yes, I realize my children are gifts. But some days I wish I could exchange them for cash.

I only have to wait thirty more years before my daughter realizes I know what I'm talking about.

How much for the angry lawn gnome?

That's my toddler.

We don't ask for much.
Just your undivided
attention and every scrap
of patience.

-kids

You know that dream when you're trying to run but you're stuck in slow motion? Parenthood is exactly like that.

Kids.

You can't wait for them to start talking, until they do.

I've never been more needed and more ignored since becoming a mom.

To anyone else, taffy
is just candy. But to
a parent, taffy is a
heavenly little piece of
shut the fuck up for three
minutes.

People who say children
are a blessing probably
don't spend every waking
minute with them.

Dance like no one's watching and cook like someone else is cleaning up that shit.

Raising children takes
a village, preferably one
with many vineyards.

I wish someone would threaten to put me to bed for a change.

Maybe mama duck
isn't leading her babies;
maybe she's trying to
outrun them.

Some of my best
memories are naps.

What doesn't kill you doesn't make you stronger, it wakes you up early on the weekend and demands pancakes.

32

People who say to take care of yourself first so you can take care of others don't understand how kids work.

I met a teenager today and now my daughter's not allowed to become one.

Once upon a time I could complete a sentence and then I had kids. The end.

Nobody ever tells you how much of being a parent is just yelling empty threats.

It's easy to go incognito when you're a mom.

Just wash your hair and put on real pants.

She died doing not what she loved, but what she did best: yelling at the kids to stop yelling.

Chips are not only delicious, but if you crunch them loud enough you can't hear your children anymore.

What's that thing called where you never sit down again?

Oh yeah, parenthood.

40

Almost everything in parenthood is way easier said than done.

The family that stares
at electronic devices
together, stays together.

You can have a good morning or you can get your kids to school on time, but you can't have both.

I'll give you 5 minutes to yourself, but only 10 seconds at a time.

-kids

I don't get parents who let their kids win—beating them at games is the only joy I have left.

45

If taking a flask to a kid's birthday party is wrong, then that's just too bad.

This too shall pass is just a polite way of saying you're screwed for now.

Let's call this family vacation what it really is: a mistake.

If you've ever said to yourself, I wish I could explain every move I make to someone all day long, then having kids is for you.

Parenting wouldn't be so hard if I didn't care how my kids turned out.

I could win the lottery, and the joy wouldn't compare to the joy of finally putting my kids to bed.

The only thing to do when your child tells you to be quiet is to sing even louder.

I love when my kids are quiet. Those ten seconds a day are priceless.

All I'm saying is you never see someone driving a minivan and smiling.

I wonder what it's like to live in a house that's not one giant junk drawer.

If you tell a parent to go to their happy place, don't be surprised when they go back to bed.

Nothing says you're a parent like being jealous of a tree because it's all alone.

Only in parenthood is the question, "Do you want more toast?" answered with, "I have to poop."

At some point, every parent gets frustrated with their kids, but what matters is how well we hide it from them.

My life as a parent is less Mary Poppins and more Shawshank Redemption.

My kids play games just like I parent: they have no idea what they're doing, and they make up everything as they go.

Telling a parent not to worry is as pointless as telling a child to be reasonable.

Before kids, you want drinks.

After kids, you *need* drinks.

Some people jump out of planes for a rush. I open candy right in front of my kids.

Eventually every parent reaches the "it's a good thing they're so cute" stage.

If the lights are all on but nobody's home, it's probably 'cause my kids were there.

I want your help, but only after I've ignored all your offers and you're busy doing something else.

-kids

98% of parenting is picking up stuff off the floor, and the other 2% is yelling about all the stuff on the floor.

That moment your daughter says she's going to smite her sister, and you're worried but proud of her word choice.

You never know what's
going on behind closed
doors unless you're
a parent then you're
probably secretly eating.

Being a parent is feeling like you're twenty minutes late even when you don't have anywhere to be.

The longer you're a parent, the harder it is to act excited when people tell you they're pregnant.

I never take advice
from anyone with kids,
because obviously they
make terrible decisions.

Being a parent is making everything easier for your kids while your kids do the exact opposite for you.

The joy of a kid on Christmas morning ain't got nothing on the joy of a parent on Back to School morning.

Why did the parents cross the road?

To get to the liquor store on the other side.

I would've gotten a Roomba long ago if I knew it'd make my kids go in the other room and shut the door.

Make sure your kids know they deserve the world, but they're not entitled to it.

Nobody needs a Fitbit
to count 10,000 steps.
All they need is a couple
kids who want breakfast.

Hell hath no fury like a child with an unanswered question.

Parenthood took away my sanity but replaced it with the craziest kind of love.

Nobody around here appreciates all the effort it takes to not run away each day.

Imagine a rest stop bathroom.
Now imagine a Denny's. Mix the two together and that's what life with kids smells like.

There's nothing like holding a baby to remind you that you don't want another one.

Having kids has taught me that I wouldn't last more than two minutes in a police interrogation.

Parenthood is an endless
roller coaster ride from
LOL to FML.

Pretty sure suffering is defined as waiting ten minutes with a child who doesn't understand how time works.

On bad days I like to take a pregnancy test to remind myself that things could be much worse.

If I didn't know better, I'd swear my kids came up with the phrase "Never take no for an answer."

That little line on your kid's sock will eventually ruin your whole day, but congratulations on your pregnancy!

I woke up in such a good mood and then I remembered I have kids.

I don't homeschool my kids 'cause the only historic battle I know is the one between Biggie and Tupac.

It's like this and like that and like this and uh it's like that and like this and like that and uh it's like this...

-my kid telling a story

Raising kids is like fighting zombies; there's no time to rest, and if you let your guard down, they eat you alive.

I don't believe in spanking my children, but I do believe in flipping them off from the other room.

Parenthood is a journey, except it's just traveling from room to room putting away the same toys all day long.

Most of being a parent is listening to people tell you to enjoy whatever crappy stage of parenthood you're currently enduring.

Everyone's taken care of except me.

Yay parenthood.

I just found out school starts a day sooner than I thought, so this must be what walking on sunshine feels like.

Marriage is where you learn the art of ignoring; parenthood is where you master it.

Parenting is mostly just watching your kids eat foods you wish you could still eat.

My parenting book is just a bottle of vodka with a post-it that says, "Drink this."

Parenting is all about balance, especially when you're chasing them with a full glass of wine in your hand.

Randomly yell out "Be careful!"

Parenting is easy!

All parenting comes down to is stepping on shit that hurts your feet.

The great thing about kids is when you don't have the answers, you make them up and they believe you.

Have kids so at least you have an excuse for never finishing anything you start.

Kids have this special
way of making you feel
hungover even when
you're not.

My kid learned how to whistle.

Send wine.

Parenting is easy as long as you sleep when the baby sleeps and wine when the children whine.

If Hansel and Gretel were my kids, they would've left a trail of wine corks instead of bread crumbs.

I know my kids will grow up and think I'm crazy. I just hope it's the good kind they'll want to be around every now and then.

The only reason to have more than one kid is so they'll raise each other while you drink wine and nap.

You know you're a parent when the only wet spot in bed is from a leaky sippy cup.

According to toddler law, anything you say can and will be used against you and repeated at the most inappropriate times.

If you had to hear your name repeated 3,457 times a day, you'd probably be crazy too.

My reasons to live are my same reasons to drink.

If I see you all smiling
and happy I'm going
to assume you're not
married, childless, and
that you got laid this
morning while eating
bacon.

It's when you see yourself in your children that you really start to worry for their future.

The hard part is not getting your kids to listen, it's trying not to strangle them when they don't.

It's not fair that kids want to help when they're the least helpful and don't want to help when they'd actually be useful.

I swear I'm not drunk, officer. Just swerving trying to get whatever my kid dropped so she'll stop screaming.

You know you're a parent when you think four hours of uninterrupted sleep is a luxury.

I want what any parent wants: for my kids to grow up to be happy and that they know how to use sarcasm.

A good day as a parent is when you only want to give up five times instead of ten.

It's not fair how parents drink all the coffee but the caffeine goes straight to the kids.

The most important parenting class is the one where you learn to play the world's smallest violin.

Most of parenting is just spelling words out loud.

For someone who isn't allowed to sit down, you'd think I'd be much skinnier.

Motherhood: side effects may include irrational mood swings, a fat ass, drunkenness, and insanity.

Childbirth was a breeze compared to this tornado of motherhood.

Parenthood is funny with a capital FU.

Kids are magical. They can make ten minutes feel like ten hours.

One minute it's fine to put your stuff on the curb with a free sign, and the next it's all "Ma'am, you can't leave your kids here."

I'm imposing a travel ban on my kids from entering the bathroom while I'm in there.

People who love cooking probably don't have to keep kids from killing each other while they do it.

Mmm hmming my way through parenthood one repetitive question at a time.

I judge my day based on how many times I threaten to take my kids to the orphanage.

You're not dying, you're just a parent.

Remember before kids
how you could do things
uninterrup

Acknowledgments

To my husband,
thank you for laughing at my dumb jokes.

To my daughters,
thank you for inspiring me to write dumb jokes.

To my parents, thank you for everything.

To my brothers, thank you for making me one of the guys.

To my friends, thank you for laughing with me.

To The Court Poet, thank you for telling me to write this.

To Caselli, thank you for helping me find the errors.

About the Author

Jewel Nunez aka One Funny Mummy has been defining parenthood in 140 characters or less since 2014. When she's not being a mom to her two girls, she's writing about being a mom to her two girls. She lives in whine country with her onefunnyfamily who always keep her laughing.

For more laughs, visit @OneFunnyMummy on Twitter, Facebook, and Instagram.

Made in the USA
San Bernardino, CA
09 December 2017